THIS BOOK BELONGS TO

. . . .

THE TALE OF
THE TOWN MOUSE
&
THE COUNTRY MOUSE
A MODERN RETELLING

First published 2006 by
Old Street Publishing Ltd, 14 Bowling Green Lane, London EC1R 0BD, UK
www.oldstreetpublishing.co.uk

ISBN: 1-905847-00-9   ISBN13: 978-1-905847-00-6

Printed in Italy by Graphicom srl

THE TALE OF
THE TOWN MOUSE
&
THE COUNTRY MOUSE

A MODERN RETELLING

BY
BEN ILLIS
WITH ILLUSTRATIONS BY
ALEXANDER SCARFE

ONCE upon a time there lived a
Town Mouse ...

... and a Country Mouse.

THE Town Mouse lived with his foster mother, Red, in a little hole under some broken down concrete steps.

... a little hole

... with his gun bug Spot

THE Country Mouse lived in a hollow tree stump with his gun bug Spot by the side of a beautiful wood only a mile or so from the local pub.

NOW the Town Mouse was a naughty mouse. Not exactly a bad mouse, but a very naughty one. He had already received three ASBOs and Red was beginning to wonder what to do with him.

He had already received three ASBOs

... dealing class C cheese in the playground

ONE day he was excluded from school for dealing class C cheese in the playground. Red was very angry.

"I 'ave 'ad it up to 'ere wiv you, you little toerag," she shouted. "I'm sendin' you to stay wiv your cousin the Country Mouse to see if you can't learn some manners!"

"Whatever," replied the Town Mouse.

MEANWHILE, the Country Mouse was enjoying a pint of foamy ale in the pub, which was very busy as usual. Hunched over a pint in the corner was a drunken newt with reddened eyes, and at the fruit machine stood a saggy looking bear, with a well chewed dog-end hanging from the corner of his mouth. A rather matronly hedgehog was serving drinks and huge wedges of cheese.

*... at the fruit machine stood a
saggy looking bear*

They've only bloody banned
stag beetle hunting!

ALL of a sudden, in stormed Amos the badger, waving a note in his paw.

"Have you seen this?" he yelled, "They've only bloody banned stag beetle hunting!"

A deathly hush descended on the room. Amos fixed his beady gaze on the Country Mouse.

INDEED, the eyes of every creature in the pub did their slightly squiffy best to focus on the Country Mouse, who thought he'd better rise to the occasion. Taking a last sip of his drink, he spoke up in his best church voice.

"For years they've been stamping on our traditional ways of life," he began. "Well, enough is enough! We can't let those blasted townies run our lives. We need to bloody well show 'em that we country folk won't be dictated to any more!"

... slightly squiffy

Jolly good show!

THERE was uproar. Cries of "Hear! Hear!" and "Jolly good show!" and "Don't you be spillin' moi point!" reverberated around the pub, as the Country Mouse was hoisted up onto swaying shoulders and carried triumphantly (if a mite unsteadily) from the room.

NEVER a great one for respecting boundaries, the Town Mouse was having a jolly good go at picking his cousin's lock, when up stormed the mouse himself.

"Whassat! You there! Have at you!" he blustered.

"Easy cuz, it's only me. Your cousin, remember? I've come to crash for a bit," replied the scruffy young mouse.

"Crash?" replied the Country Mouse suspiciously. "Into what, may I ask?"

Whassat? You there? Have at you!

*... against the Country Mouse's
better judgement*

"CRASH. As in 'doss', 'kip' - er - 'sleep'..."

"What, here?!" exclaimed the Country Mouse in horror. "Out of the question. I'm just off to the smoke. The real question is, where should I 'crash'?"

"You could always kip round my gaff, while I look after yours. Go on! I'm sure my foster Mum'd love the company."

And so, against the Country Mouse's better judgement, the question of crashing, dossing, kipping or sleeping was decided.

A short while later the Country Mouse was in a taxi, his Gentlemouse's valise neatly packed next to him. As they drove past two teams of crickets playing cricket on the village green, he realised there was something familiar about his driver. Those greenish gills, that mustard cravat...

"Toad...?!"

*... crickets playing cricket on
the village green*

"Oh dash it all!" replied Toad

"WHAT on earth are you doing driving a taxi cab?" exclaimed the Country Mouse.

"Oh dash it all!" replied Toad (for it was he). "Times have been a bit tough don'tcha know. After the paw and mouth scare I had to get rid of my beetle herds, and now there's this gnat flu. I don't know what I'm going to do when they bring in the hunting ban. My hunting wasps are just about all I have left."

"Now that is exactly why I am off to the city. Going to have a word with the old MP..."

"Good on you mouse old chap!" cried Toad, swerving to avoid an old shrew on her bicycle, who was no doubt spreading a spot of malicious gossip and living in hope - as all elderly village spinsters do - of one day solving a murder or two over a nice cup of Earl Grey and a slice of Battenberg cake.

... swerving to avoid an old shrew
on her bicycle

He began to rummage

THE Town Mouse, meanwhile, had thoroughly explored his cousin's hole, and was getting bored.

Suddenly, he had a marvellous idea. A grin spread across his whiskered face. He scurried over to his Adimouse kit bag, and began to rummage. Then, stuffing something into the pocket of his hoodie, he marched purposefully out of the stump.

NEARBY, a herd of cows were busy standing around for all they were worth. The Town Mouse took out a can of spray paint and, with a flick of the wrist, tagged one with his trademark 'SKWEEK'.

Then the naughty mouse set off down the path towards the village, sniggering.

"How rude!" thought the cow, and chewed the cud a little more indignantly.

"How rude!" thought the cow

Don't get many of those back home!

THE Country Mouse descended from his train, and approached a porter to ask for directions.

"Iss my break, innit," replied the porter in a thick accent, turning his back.

"Ruddy unhelpful," thought the Country Mouse. "And a most peculiar looking rodent, to boot. Don't get many of those back home!"

Drawing his Gentlemouse's valise mistrustfully to his waist, he made his way towards the station exit.

BACK in the country, the Town Mouse was getting rather hungry. Knowing there was no more cheese at home - he had polished it all off earlier in a fit of munchies - he set to foraging in the hedgerow.

Suddenly, there was a deafening crash. A huge shape descended towards him as if from nowhere, razor-sharp talons extended...

"FUCK ME!" squeaked the little mouse.

"Fuck me!" squeaked the little mouse

"Whatever, granddad," retorted
one of the little mouselings

UNAWARE of his cousin's peril, the Country Mouse was having difficulties of his own. In short, he was lost.

Nearby, a litter of young mice were huddled sullenly round one of their number, who was proudly demonstrating a very flashy mobile telephone.

"What ho!" called the Country Mouse, but they appeared not to have heard. "I say, chaps!" he called out again.

"Whatever, granddad," retorted one of the little mouselings, making the others giggle.

THE Country Mouse's blood began to boil.

"Come here!" he bellowed. The mouseling approached sulkily, arms crossed. "In my day we treated our elders with respect!" said the Country Mouse.

Kissing his teeth, the mouseling replied, "Thing is, granddad, the way I see it, your day is long gone."

The Country Mouse realised he was completely surrounded by little mouselings, some of whom had produced makeshift bats which they were brandishing very menacingly indeed.

... completely surrounded by
little mouselings

Fuck fuck fuck fuck fuck FUCK!

THE owl missed the Town Mouse by less than a whisker.

"Fuck fuck fuck fuck fuck FUCK!" he thought, as, heart pounding in his little ears, he ran for his life towards the pub.

THE Town Mouse threw himself through the door of the pub with a crash. He was breathing so hard it took him a minute to realise that every creature in the room was staring at him. A booming voice broke the silence.

"You made me miss the board!"

A burly rabbit dressed in a blue coat stepped threateningly forward, clutching some darts. All the other creatures eyed him nervously.

"I haven't missed the board in years," he continued.

You made me miss the board!

Leave 'im alone you little toerags!

MEANWHILE the ambushed Country Mouse was also in a spot of bother. Just as he was starting to think he was done for, there was an ear-splitting screech.

"OI! Leave 'im alone you little toerags!"

The owner of the screech came thundering over to the ringleader of the mouselings, who scampered away in terror (but not before getting a sharp cuff round the ear).

The Country Mouse breathed a sigh of relief, then looked up to take in the enormity of his saviour.

"I'M ever so sorry 'bout that. You ok?" she said.

"Erm. Yes, quite alright thank you. A little shaken, but otherwise fine. Um...er...I wonder if you might help me? I...er...I'm trying to...ahem...that is...find a...a lady by the name of Red," stammered the Country Mouse.

I'm trying to find a lady
by the name of Red ...

And I don't do no discounts!

"WELL then it's your lucky day, 'cos you just found 'er," replied Red (for it was she), licking her lips suggestively. "This a recommendation? Only I don't get many of them. And I don't do no discounts!"

"LEAVE it, Pete," warned Amos the badger, as the bunny in blue advanced towards the Town Mouse. Without breaking eye contact, the rabbit backed off.

"Some kind of nutter is 'e?" the Town Mouse enquired, trying as hard as he could to sound casual.

The badger glared at him.

"Erm, got any cheese?" the little mouse managed to ask.

Some kind of nutter is 'e?

Cheese is off

"CHEESE is off," answered the badger firmly.

The Town Mouse looked around the room at the many varieties of cheese being enjoyed by the other customers.

"Oh. 'S'like dat is it?" he said, regaining his confidence.

The badger continued to stare.

"Fine. Well fuck you too," squeaked the enraged mouse.

And, spinning on his paws, he stormed out of the pub.

"COME on love," cooed Red, "Let Li'l Red Ridin' 'ood 'elp you get a load off."

She puckered up and made a grab for the horrified Country Mouse.

"What's that? Well, I mean to say!" he squealed in panic.

Then, abandoning both his valise and his chivalry, he fled back down the road.

Let Li'l Red Ridin' 'ood
'elp you get a load off

OUTSIDE the pub, the Town Mouse was very angry indeed. "Fuck dis!" he muttered, as he left the country folk a little present on the doorstep, "I is goin' 'ome."

SAFELY around the corner from the predatory Ms Hood, the Country Mouse considered his predicament. "Dash it all!" he cried. "I am going home."

AND so they did.

AND whenever anyone asked about their trips they would smile and reply: "Well, the grass is certainly not greener on the other side."

BUT of course we all know it used to be much greener on both.

THE END